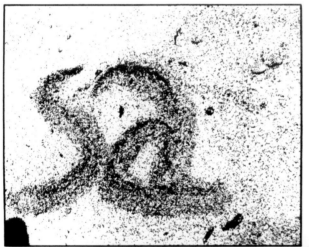

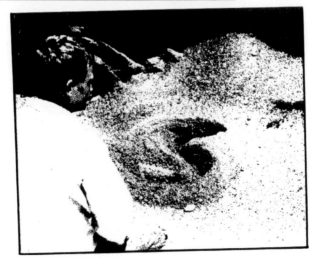

A DAY AT THE BEACH

Robert Grenier

for the six directions

5th printing 2022
Copyright © 1984, 2022 by Robert Grenier

Photographs thanks to Donald Guravich
Production by Diane Ward

ISBN: 978-1-937804-14-8
Library of Congress Catalog Card Number: 2008935479

Roof Books are distributed by
Small Press Distribution
1341 Seventh Street
Berkeley, CA. 94710-1409
Phone orders: 800-869-7553
www.spdbooks.org

Roof Books are published by
Segue Foundation
300 Bowery
New York, NY 10012-2802
seguefoundation.com

A DAY AT THE BEACH

Robert Grenier

MORNING

WANDERING ORIGIN OF SWEETPEAS

warm & grassy sounding space basis

just _beautiful_ from hunger bees

once in a while who just scattered seeds

CRAVE

crack

w i t h o u t e n   a n y   d o u b t e

APPROACHING #(OCEAN WATER

if the wind rises & it never rains

that one tire has to be balanced

but it's better than it was at fifty

WE'RE MOVING

v'ere moving ve go <u>aha</u> <u>ha</u>

OFF THE BRIM
    <u>for</u> <u>Tom</u> <u>Raworth</u>

need to have

this hat on cause

the sun is getting

awfully bright

SWIMMING

reflection part

bears me up

genuine risk

surface

seems so much more

you sink hard than land

shiny

TODAY

today

DAWN

what was

the night

more behind

EMIL NOLDE

noch einmal

SINCE THOUGHT

is the foliage of the mind I think

that thought inheres in vines

EVER A BOUNDLESS SURFACE

like almost soundless warm

blue is blue

shoes off hear

the airplane passing

up there to

MICKEY MOUSE

is Mrs. Meikles

TERRITORIAL

so what that they're over there

that's right that they're over there

they can be there

ok

REMARKABLY CLOUDLESS

out to sea except for so far

METER

would be the shape
if getting the shirt on
backwards
if getting it on

if taking it off
armholes headhole frontwards
rightsideout
backwards would be the back

OVERHEAD

where's that plane empty

THAT CAR MUST NEVER MOVE

and when it does

you were in a better humor

getting out does

SPACES

spaces solids those are spaces too

DECENT

rings am

exercise

RHYTHM

constant

motion flies

fleas dare

what

DIGGING

that's the

grave of a seal

very

nice

Boom

KATHLEEN O

"do"   "see"

COLOR

color of the sea for that

A ROAD IN THE BRUSH

a road goes by

bounded by brush

on both sides

next the pitch of the slope

downwards gone to seed

deep green far side

NOT TO BE

not to be comfortably whom

HI SEAL

hi seal

hello seal

SHOE FROM THE WAVES

oh he got a shoe from the waves

FLIES

are actually moving along or moving along

X

ex

tremely quiet

at low tide

BOOM

swims the

fleas must be going crazy

resituate

BOOM

another

earthworks

fortification

well that's four

CRYSTAL

I think that's what happens to Crystal

white and black sports

CLOUDS THE MILKY WAY

vertebrate see it as bones

I CAN'T

I can't talk and
look out the window
and talk at
the same time

& QUIET

rain now
too dark &
cold it
settles principally

rain now
too dark
and cold
it snows

FAIR THROUGH THURSDAY

light that
trawler appears
close <u>n</u>
dark

WHATSOEVER

several of'm

OF

begun

THE WHIRLIGIG

the whirligig
around & around
whirred

that
whirled
whirl

whirl
that
whirled

FOG IN BUSHES

   for _Robt_. _Creeley_

thirty feet away _a_

film on

bluish _grey_

I can trust my eyes

HELP HELP

it's foggy foggy foggy foggy

help help it's foggy

BEACH TICK

I render you lifeless

with my bare hands you don't

crawl up out from

under a ton of sand

INDOORS IN AN OFFICE AWFUL OWWW

woman laborer shovelling asphalt tar

STAY ALL DAY MEANING

I don't want to go anywhere

trawler is looping tanker

is heading south

how many dark meat eaters do we have here

c o u p l a   a p p l e s

MAN ALONG THE RED HAIR SEA SHORE

people would almost more likely be murderers than not

DOESN'T FOLLOW

walnut pieces

signal climate folly

it's colder now

such a beautiful dog

PELICANS

Pelicans they eat fish there are fish

CIVILIZATION BEACH USE VARIOUS

oh glad it's tentacles
so much to do at
low tide hunting gathering

societies have big
emancipated from the land
see each other up

above the horizon twitching
sent us out con-
solidated diversified

BOOM

loping in the direction of the bird

a quarter of a mile away out

to sea on those rocks

THEORY / GULLS FLY

north when it's clear

south when it's cloudy

TRAPEZOID

they fish in a square

HELP HELP

   <u>for</u> <u>Larry</u>

it's foggy

gas is pouring out

on the street

with nothing around

AIRPLANE FAR AWAY

not long for your helicopter

good spirals

vvisited by feather white

PISSES

belches spreading back problems

PURPLE

seashore funny greenish black

interest in tissue what

makes people so interesting

AND A

nobody knows what the and stands for today

territorial prison for the reverend moon

ROUND

& about

gracefully

eventually

this bag here

tends to dis-

courage the wind

BEACH CLOUDS

what are the figures

that come off the horizon

'backwards'

west to east

FOG OVER SUNSHINE INLAND

singular passage of time to time

still remember heat of the day

while coat on & visual evidence

remainder everything is grey

PULSE

how big a gap can a line contain & go on

TAKEN

this is the form that I've taken

MOURNING DOVES APART

mourning doves a part
that he or she gainful
to drive downtown
to hear small planes

ROW OF EUCALYPTUS

staring at those trees not with the last

(heat) light in them but day's today's

they go into shadow equably if moodily

terror could be their standing on to wave

MOON

in the afternoon

less than half layering

in the blue sky seeping

to shine tonight

THE OLD MOON WITH THE NO MOON IN HER ARMS RISING

the new quarter moon sea light has the afternoon sky

WINDOW BLOWING IN THE FOG AT SEVEN

window blowing in the fog at seven

that the palm leaves should rustle

in the foreignness of their look

MIDDAY

GAZES / GAEA

a second afternoon

press up thumb with scalp to open spout

IT'S A STORMY DAY IN CALIFORNIA

watching the ship raining out to sea

BLUE SKIES

if the wind keeps blowing light breeze perfect temperature prime of life

                    BOOM

                    sees a bird out so far away

                    shadow overhead

                    blacking by mad maddens the run

                         AFF AFF

                         arf arf

                         arf arf aff aff

CAR

can't depend on the auto

mobile as substitute

for some sort of <u>self</u>-<u>concept</u>

IRENE

one "I" stress on the first syllable

CONTEMPT

can't depend on the auto

mobile as some kind of substitute

for adequate <u>self</u>-<u>contempt</u>

HAND

missing sixth finger

space between index finger & the thumb

large enough as void to counterbalance

missing digit mass between #1

& thumb between the two in length & non-

existent consort of the little one

SURF

silence of wave formations

regardless of rocks

SURFACE

if it moves it emerges at last on top of the sand

CARCASSE

I want to see it

I don't see it

h l e a p s o b l i g h t s

BLUE SKY

for Kathleen Frumkin

over green veldt

blue water

BUT AND SEA QUARTER SALT SAND

glint of the sunshine off the glare of the waves

FUCK

owww

SIT HERE NAKED

time to do that

when I first arrived

but it's warm enough now

with the wind & the page

I've been so happy

KATHLEEN

I talked to Rin-<u>tin</u>-Tin

FRESH WATER

the little watercourse

sands into

the greater water

LIFE

for Norman & Joanne

no minded no flower completely

but yet not yet numb

not a fly anyway strum

U Y N G E U Y G N U K P H

s c e n i c

THOUGHTLESS DOTH

change shoes

MARCH SUNSHINE FOLLOWED BY WIND & SHADE

   for Marcia Lawther

all of the yellow flowers of the sour grass closed

THING I LIKED

about Portland

Oregon it was

rainy a lot

& roses &

now it's ashen

why nlo

WRITING INSTRUMENT

warmth of the page

with the fingers in hand

SHAPES

shape only

subadjacent to

chaos expanding

forming shapes

FOOL

madman though ye beem

PROLIFERATING RAW DATA

rising level of generalization

abandoned object actually except as example

BUUUHH

end of the next

shift the

smoke stacking

the steamstack

the swing shift

getting off

WHY IS MY MOTHER DEAD

for timeless grieving

HAPPY KATHLEEN

E E E U G U H H

E U G U H H O O O

slepen al the yë with melodye ya

FINCHES

chicken yesterday no beef chicken beef chicken

GOOD DOG

no woof no no

no woof no

FEELING COLDER SWEATER HAT

there is a real sequence of clothes

STANDS

sea a green

ish rock back

sands to enjoy

the late afternoon

BOOM

cracks

the nut eats

peanuts but

not the shell

grateful for the parting of the clouds

then when the rainfall falls again

COTTAGE DARK BEHIND

I think this weekend they've gone

SILHOUETTE

you have to do the work

that the boat is doing

& you have to go

in the direction that the boat is going

THREAT

from the

pounding sea

if ever

to say back

ho hum he's a scatterashoe
ho hum he's a scatterashoe
ho hum he's a scatterashoe
ho hum he's a scatterashoe

PESTS

those little flies

scrab the water

even if I can hear it

SHOULDN'T BE

all this time it's been

polished by the water

action of the waves

KATHLEEN

I would charge a quarter &

I should bear a grudge

CLOUDS

take on

the shape coming

up off the horizon

from the shadows

back here

WISH IT WAS ME

or me

FOR WALTER PATER

Well! something of the effect

if not the result of

marijuana is gained by smoking

my own home-grown weed

PLACE TO SEE

eyeballs

from getting baked

THOTH

and so the tuft

the tuft after all these years

TWO

out to make

one bird high

above spiralling

southward

water

MOVE OVER

here where I can

see the water

even if not hear it

WATCHING

pushing waves way up here

MILD

but that the wind doesn't reeve it

latc afternoon

        LAG

        ahh

        wave

        grey as

        the grave

LIGHT SHINING BEHIND THE CLOUD

sun disappeared & then

grey cloud drew cold

sat down muttering

bright sun shone

BOOM

I never

saw you big

clumsy bound

ding dog

build up solution patterns from the right side

PISSING

for Kenneth Irby

always excellent

employment for the eyes

THROUGH THE BARN

seeing where the sky

now I think it's a white door

TIDE GOING DOWN

quieter sky later I noticed

SEAL LOOKS ASHORE

from the surf much like a human

creature like that in the water swims scans

much like the dog in better days on land

NO MORE BREAD ON THE END OF THE TABLE

what's that I hear being sunq

BOOM

dug rather remarkably large

holes in the sand today

SUNNY BRRR

shoes on a sweater

PLEASANT

supportive through the day

sleep in the sun warmest

spot latest in the day

turn around & face the sea says I

I

swam again

when the

shade disappears

I must go

AFTERNOON / EVENING

THEY'VE

wind today the pelicans have have it

AYE

that means some distance

hours come

DOWN THE ROAD ABEND

   for Anselm

some of this stuff comes from a

collaboration that now seems all enthusiasm

FAVORITE MOON

in the Redwoods

SWOLLEN

was sunshine

alone

CANNISTER

nice little aerosol of sprays

B O A T S

boats always appear against the horizon

STAND UP SEE

shooting stars

from the inside

flies on the outside

dot the visual field

BOAT A

scow with trucks

FISH OVER THERE

owww

look now

again

                        .

ANYBODY

was going to stop out there

SLAP

to the

thigh a little slow

REGARDFUL OF MASSES

stay here for four hours

LEAVES

the wind makes good the trees

determination to go walking

would take me from home

I search for my hat and stand

allied investigatory airplane

BODIES AGAIN

look just like Mrs. Meikles

NUNS AT SHORE

one night
one of the older
nuns looked out
into the courtyard
and saw
another nun
whom she did not
immediately know

GREEN CAR

to helicopter

on the cliff must be

a regular phenomenon passing

as they are to me

NEXT HAT

other hat

ma mind

my mind mine

BURNING

the ground free of particles

FLAPPING BY FLAPPING THE ARMS

I couldn't remember to go up or back up to find it

there is a lot of storms

there are a lot of storms

POISON OAK

don't dwell
on de gap between
knuckles bubbles are
bubbling up

TREATMENT

wants to take its course never

mind treatment

FLIES CHALLENGING

everything anybody

might be saying

MAYBE I SHOULD EAT

the sandwich I

brought for myself

SPAWNED BY THE FOAM INTELLIGENCE

the monster goes back into the sea

or such sludge as remains for it

ugh matter more akin by rockhard doing

to the origin of things than Dr. Frankenstein

TWO ENGINE

petrol plane tarts the lot of them

AGAINST SILENCE

melody

not versus

if an apple fell on your skull

you would stand up & rub

the bump on your

abdomen

HERE WE HAVE

here we have a rather anonymous

piece of foam I can bring that back

BOOM THAT SLEEPS THERE RED-BROWN

feeling himself secure from the

waves & wash of its sound

by the little bank of pebbles

that protects him anon

WIND COMING UP

would disperse

any fog there was

ha ha ha ha ha hah hey you

MASSIVE

clouds of

small flies flying south

causing the yellow moon

to rise in the east

BOOM

sitting

the flies

landing on him

and biting

SEEKING ME

seeking me as figures in the terrain

                periodachbelly

VOICE SAYS

v o i c e s

SOME SAY

we should suffer through

an inflicting state

of global privation

brought on by our

misuse of nature rather than

all-out total war

CAN'T SEE TO THE TUNNEL

thick monster fog a little soggy

shapes coming in

THESE APPEAR

to be more rounded down & sought

SEA

shore

primitive

home of man

SO

that was a
decision that there
would be such a place
and that there was

THESE FLIES / FORTY

rage

at my

inefficiency

against

the speed

of

forces

MONSTERS

pick up & go

stay put fast

TWO

& two

four

three

six

seven

CONCRETE POST TO METAL SIGN

see the conceptualization is something

REVENGE

for Anselm Hollo

death for biting

crawling

five are furies of foam

SUNSHINE

for Robt. Burns

frostbite & radiation is burn

GRANDEUR

photoplay

neither wrought

apples nor

bread

nude it thing west

FORMALLY MEMORY

what would inquire into

cloud patterns formerly

in the sky

shadows the land

SUNSHINE

I think almost without limit

INCENTIVE

incentive now to

get one of them

SHOOTS

look at those roots

it's all a big vine

all tangled that's it

BEACH

I cleared it

started over pommelling

SAND AND SKY ABOVE

big strawberries

& roots of wild blue

strawberries colonizing

the surface

THE CENOTAPH

a stag in the wood crying remains

STEADY SOLID

pouring

without a

thunderclap

imagine night if you

if you could't go

in the direction that you

that you know

DUH

the harbor bings

GREEN LEAVES OF THE WALNUT

you wait so late grey sky of spring

behind to white to see them

TRAINS IN THE NIGHT / AGAIN BY DAY

instead of representing

passage of time eternity

motion along a line

still transpiring yet

trees along a watercourse

we can regard of whistles

honey touch me in the soft night

POPLAR

steam rain toward

frozen brrr

fountain branches

tower

JUG'S UP

for David Bromige

the jig's up

they're all there

SAYING

saying in advance off they go

SAXING

saying _anyway_ _I_ _don't_ _know_

THE LAW

   after _Charles_ _Bernstein_

that law
discriminates against those
(who) that have to cross (who)
(a) city street for lunch (piss)

      BORING

      vines ground

      pattern fences

      sidewalk stucco

      pouring